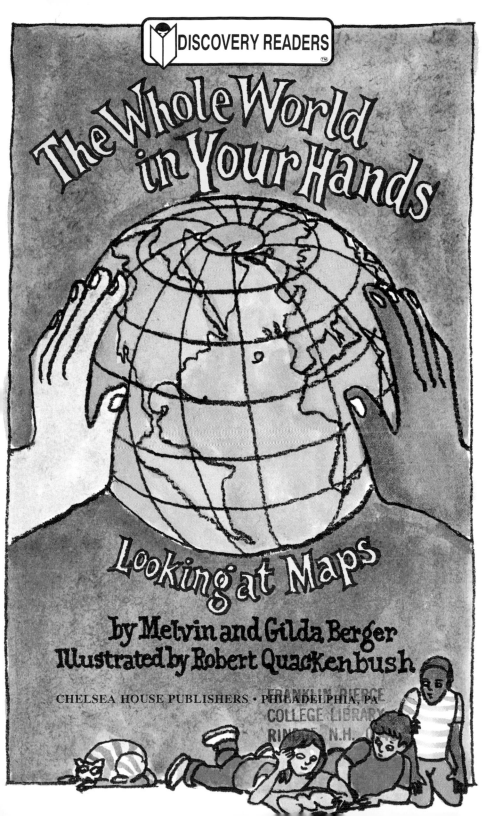

DISCOVERY READERS™

The Whole World in Your Hands

Looking at Maps

by Melvin and Gilda Berger
Illustrated by Robert Quackenbush

CHELSEA HOUSE PUBLISHERS · PHILADELPHIA, PA

The authors, artist, and publisher wish to thank the following for their invaluable advice and instruction for this book:

Jane Hyman, B.S., M. Ed. (Reading), M. Ed. (Special Needs), Ed. D. (candidate)

Rose Feinberg, B.S., M. Ed. (Elementary Education), Ed. D. (Reading and Language Arts)

R.L. 1.8 Spache

First hardback edition published by Chelsea House Publishers in 1999.

Printed and bound in Mexico.

Library of Congress Cataloging-in-Publication Data

Berger, Melvin.
   The whole world in your hands: looking at maps / by Melvin and
   Gilda Berger; illustrated by Robert Quackenbush. p. cm.—
   (Discovery readers) Includes index. Summary: Explains what maps
   are and how to use them, discusses map symbols and their
   meanings, and includes maps of a house, community, city, state,
   country, and the world.
   ISBN 0-7910-5073-4 (hc)
   1. Maps—Juvenile literature. [1. Maps.] I. Berger, Gilda. II.
   Quackenbush, Robert M., ill. III. Title. IV. Series.
   GA105.6.B47 1998
   912—dc21
                                                            98-26981
                                                               CIP
                                                               AC

Here's a map.
It's a map of the world.
The world is thousands of miles
across.
Yet it fits on this map.

Pick up the map.
Now you've the whole world in
your hands!

A map is a picture.
It shows a place as it looks from
    up high.
A map makes big distances look
    small.

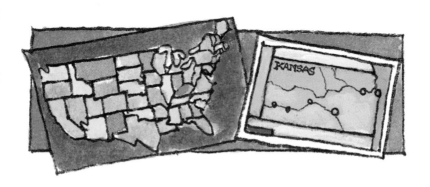

Maps may show the whole world.
Or they may show
    —one country
    —one state
    —one city
    —one community
    —even one house!

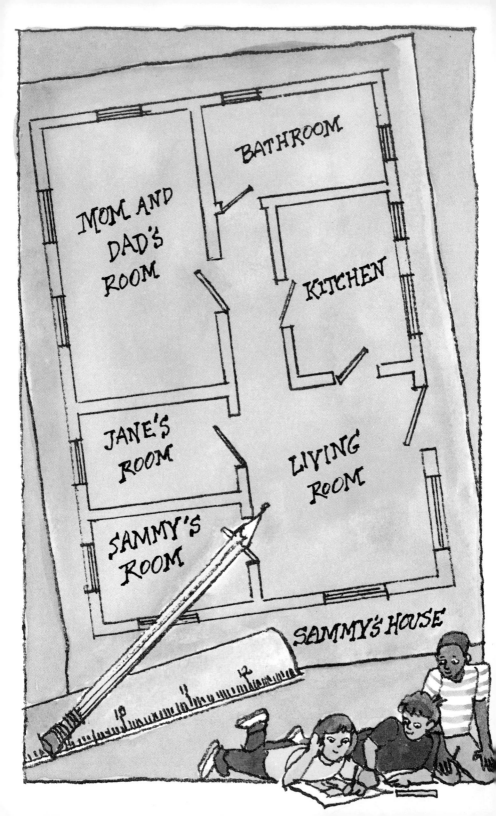

Here's a map of Sammy's house.
It shows Sammy's room.
His sister Jane's room.
Mom and Dad's room.

Whose room is near Sammy's room?
Whose room is far from Sammy's
    room?

Sammy's house has other rooms
    —a living room
    —a kitchen
    —a bathroom.

Can you find each room?

Sammy and Jane have alarm clocks.
Their alarms ring at 7:30 every
    school day.
The brother and sister race to the
    bathroom.
Each wants to be first.
Jane usually wins.
Can you see why?

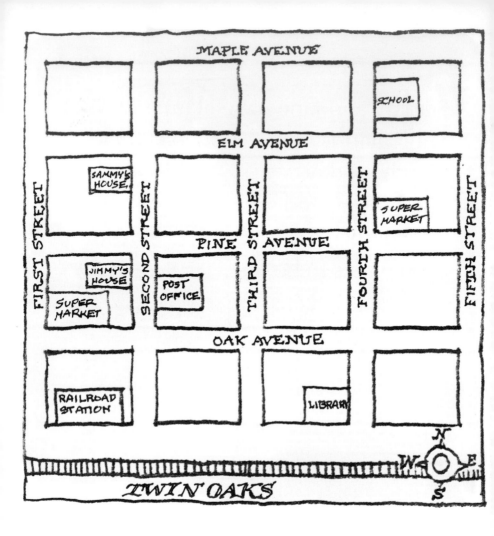

Sammy's house is in a community
    called Twin Oaks.
This is a map of his community.
Sammy's house is on Second Street.
Do you see it?

All the streets in Twin Oaks run up
and down.
Up and down on a map means
north and south.

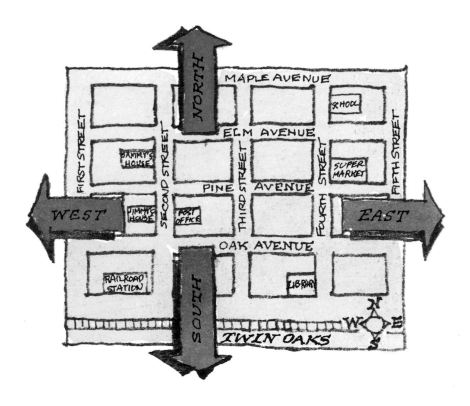

Move up on a map and you go
north.
Move down on a map and you go
south.

All the avenues run from side to
    side.
Side to side on a map means east
    and west.

Move right on a map and you go
    east.
Move left on a map and you go
    west.

Most maps have four arrows off to
    the side.
The arrows show the four directions—

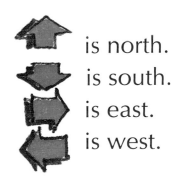 is north.
is south.
is east.
is west.

Sammy's best friend also lives on
   Second Street.
His name is Jimmy.
Jimmy lives between Pine Avenue
   and Oak Avenue.

Sammy often plays at Jimmy's
   house.
Jimmy lives south of Sammy.
To get to Jimmy's house, Sammy
   walks south on Second Street.

Sammy and Jimmy walk to school
   together.
Jimmy walks north on Second Street
   to Sammy's house.

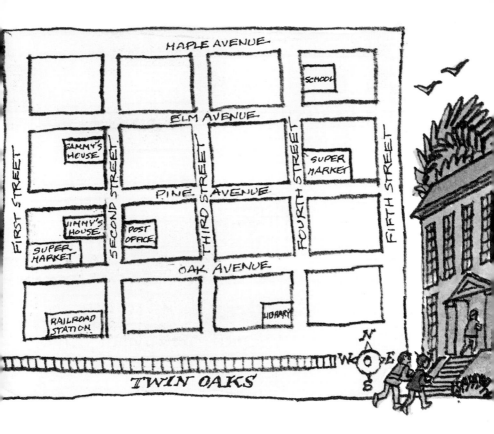

Together they go east on Elm
Avenue.
Then they turn north on Fourth
Street.
The school is right there.
Can you trace their way with your
finger?

Every Saturday Sammy goes to the
    library.
He walks south on Second Street to
    Pine Avenue.
He turns east and walks to Fourth
    Street.
At Fourth Street, he turns south.
Trace Sammy's path with your finger.

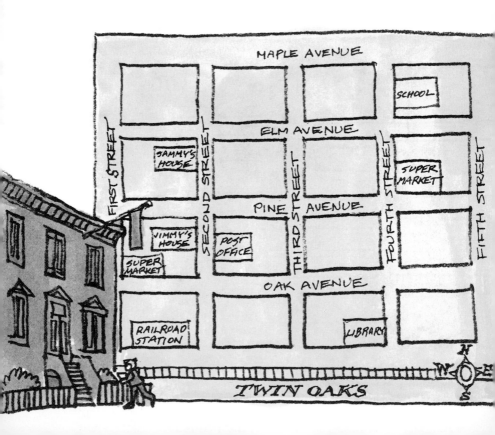

Can you figure out how Sammy
   walks
   —to the post office
   —to the railroad station
   —to the supermarket?

Twin Oaks is in a small city called
Westover.
This map shows the town's main
roads.
North Highway is north of the town.
South Highway is south.
West Highway is on the west side.
East Highway is to the east.

The map also shows some important
places in Westover
—the airport
—the fairgrounds
—the zoo
—the ballpark
—the movie theater
—two shopping malls.

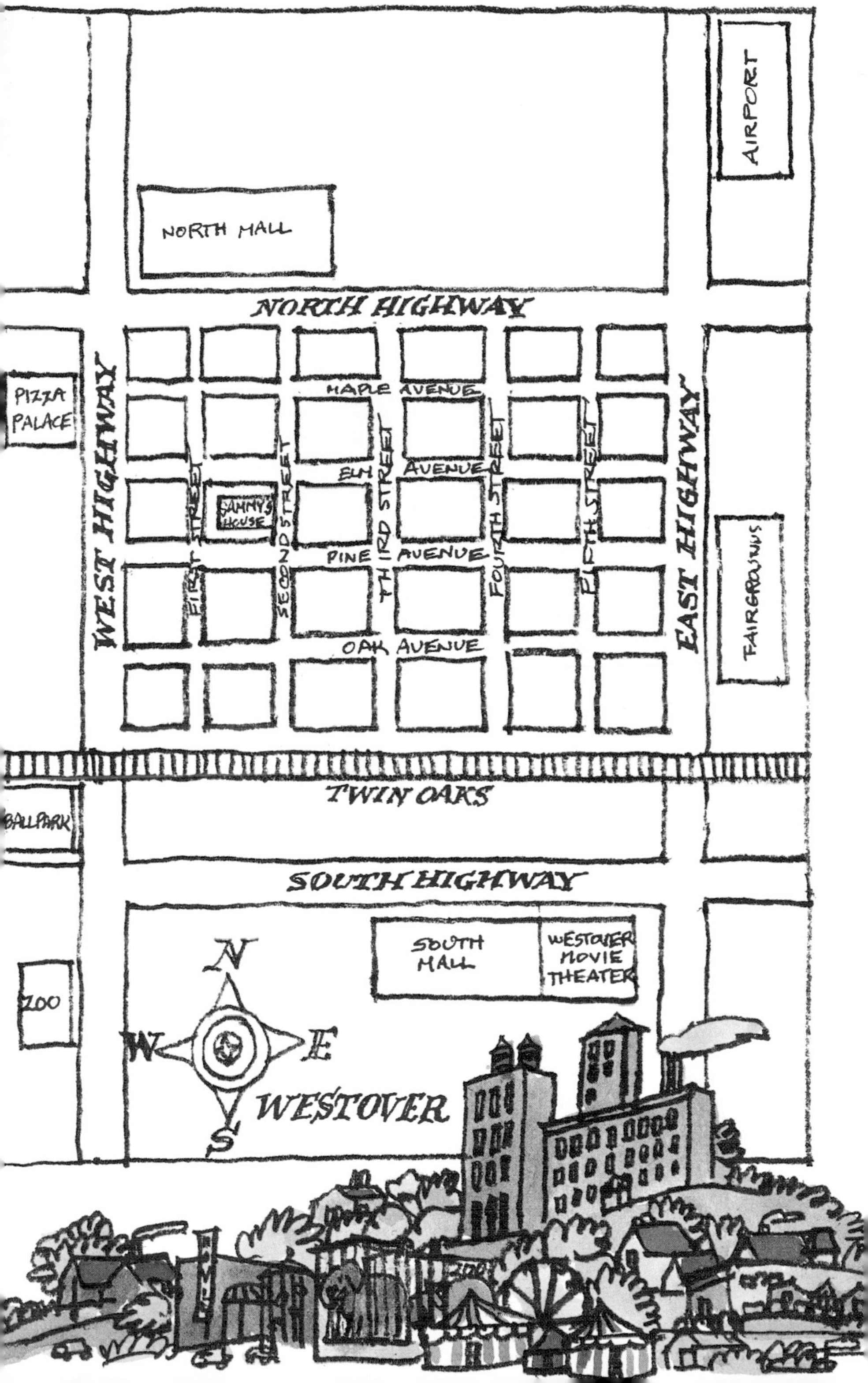

AIRPORT
NORTH MALL
NORTH HIGHWAY
PIZZA PALACE
WEST HIGHWAY
EAST HIGHWAY
MAPLE AVENUE
ELM AVENUE
PINE AVENUE
OAK AVENUE
FIRST STREET
SECOND STREET
THIRD STREET
FOURTH STREET
FIFTH STREET
SAMMY'S HOUSE
FAIRGROUNDS
TWIN OAKS
BALLPARK
SOUTH HIGHWAY
SOUTH MALL
WESTOVER MOVIE THEATER
ZOO
N
E
S
W
WESTOVER

One day Sammy's family went to the
    fairgrounds.
Sammy's mother drove.

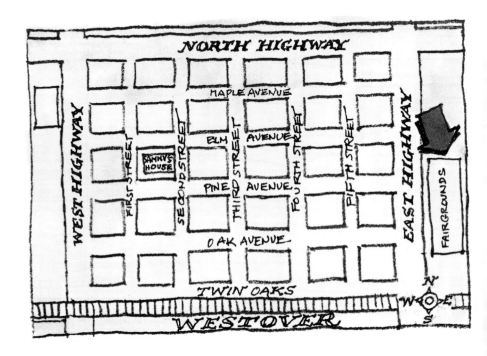

First she went east on Elm Avenue.
Then she turned south on East
    Highway.
Finally she parked at the fairgrounds.
Sammy and Jane tried all the rides.

Each summer Grandma comes to
   visit.
Sammy's dad goes to meet her.
He drives to the airport.

First Dad heads north on Second
   Street.
Next he turns east on North
   Highway.
When he gets to East Highway, he
   turns north.
He follows that road to the airport.

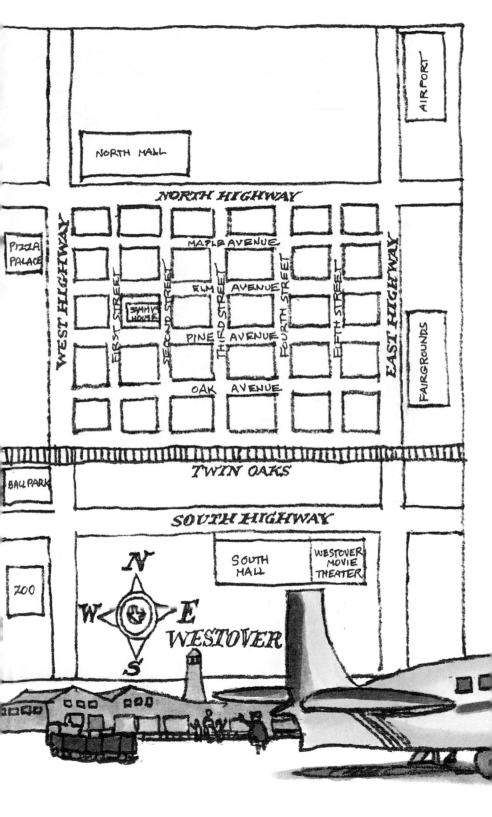

Sammy's town could be anywhere.
Let's pretend it's in the state of
    Kansas.
Kansas is right in the middle of the
    United States.

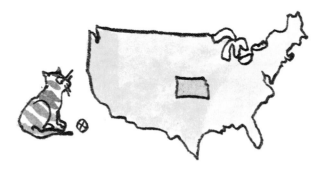

Here is a map of Kansas.
The dots show the cities.
The bigger the dot, the bigger the
    city.
Can you find three big cities in
    Kansas?
Wichita is the biggest city in Kansas.
Nearly half a million people live in
    Wichita.

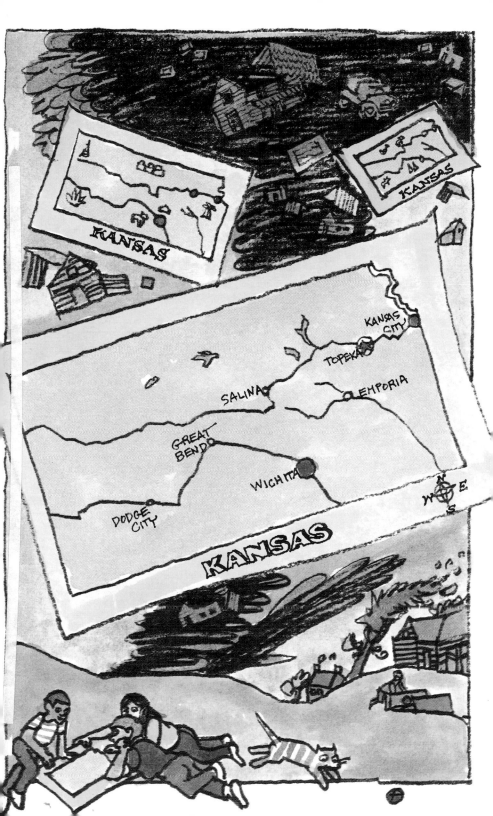

Next to the Wichita dot is a drawing
   of small airplanes in a factory.
The drawing is a symbol.
It tells you that people in Wichita
   build small airplanes.
Many people in this city work in
   airplane factories.
Others do different kinds of work.

26

Kansas City is in the northeast
   corner of Kansas.
The city is only about half as big as
   Wichita.
So Kansas City has a smaller dot on
   the map.

Topeka is just west of Kansas City.
It is the smallest of the big cities in
   Kansas.

Topeka has a star inside a dot.
A star is the symbol of a capital city.
Topeka is the capital of Kansas.

The governor of Kansas lives and
    works in Topeka.
Many others who live in Topeka also
    work for the state.

There's much more to Kansas than
    its cities.
A lot goes on in the rest of the state.

STATE MAP

Do you see the sheaves of wheat in
the west part of Kansas?
This symbol shows that farmers
grow wheat all around here.
Kansas farmers grow more wheat
than farmers in any other state.

Kansas farmers also raise chickens,
sheep, and cattle.
Look for tiny symbols of these
animals on the map.
These symbols show where you can
find most of the animal farms.

The northwest part of the map shows oil well symbols.
Lots of oil lies under the ground here.

Move south on the map.
Go to the southwest corner of Kansas.
Here you see pictures of flames.
Workers pump natural gas from this area.

Head east across the map.
Do you see little cars loaded with
    coal?
It's easy to guess what happens here.
Coal miners dig for coal in deep
    tunnels.

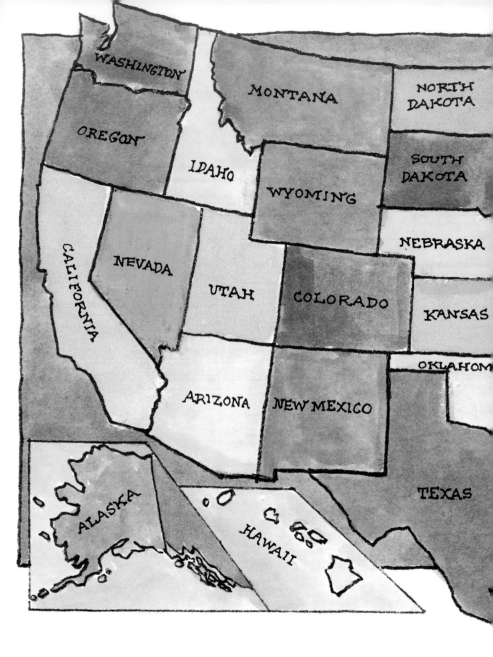

Kansas is one state in the United
    States.
The United States has fifty states.

Here is a map of our whole country.
Can you find Kansas?
Can you find your state?

There are about 150 countries in the whole world.

The countries are spread out over seven continents—Asia, Africa, North America, South America, Antarctica, Australia, and Europe.

Between the continents are four main oceans—Atlantic, Pacific, Indian, and Arctic.

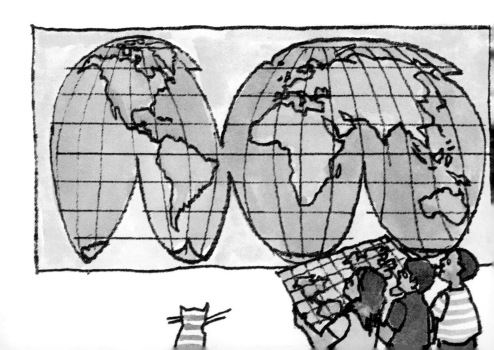

This map shows the continents and
oceans of the world.

This map is like the first map in the
book.
They are both maps of the world.
Yet there is one big difference.

The map in the front makes the
world look flat.
This map shows that the world is
round.
The world is really as round as a
globe.

An orange is also as round as a
globe.
Imagine a map of the world on the
orange skin.

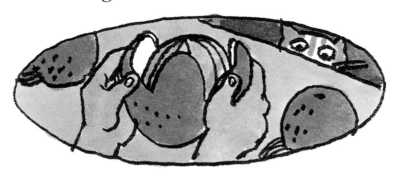

Peel off the orange skin in one big
piece.

Push the skin flat on a table.

The orange-skin map would look
like this map.

Take a close look at the map.
Can you find South America?

Find the line marked equator. It is
    like a belt around the middle of
    the world.
North of the equator is the northern
    half of the world.
South of the equator is the southern
    half of the world.

Near the equator:
    Every day is like a summer day.
    People wear light clothes to keep
        cool.
    Trees and grass and flowers grow
        all year long.
    Plants grow quickly.
    Sweet potatoes, peanuts, and
        corn grow well.

Now find the North Pole on the
    map.
It is far up in the north.

Find the South Pole.
It is far down in the south.
Did you know that the poles are the
    coldest places in the world?

Near the poles:
    Every day is cold.
    There's lots of snow and ice.
    People wear heavy clothes to
        keep warm.
    Few animals or plants live or
        grow on the land.

Here almost all living things are
    found in the seas.

Not many people live near the
poles.
And few live near the equator.

Most people live in places in
between.

In those places, the weather is
mild.
Usually it is not very hot or very
cold.
Some people live where the soil is
rich.
These places are good for farming.

Some people live near big forests.
Many cut trees for lumber.

Some people live near oceans or
   rivers.
Many catch and eat lots of seafood.

Some people live where there is oil
   under the ground.
Many drill for oil and ship it out.

Some people live in big cities.
Many work in factories and offices.

KANSAS

A map can tell many things
    —the work people do
    —the foods they eat
    —the clothes they wear
    —the kinds of houses they live in.

Maps are wonderful tools.
They help bring us all closer
       together.

Index